Wartime Teesside

by Bill Norman

Dalesman Books 1989

The Dalesman Publishing Company Ltd.,
Clapham, Lancaster, LA2 8EB

First published 1989

© Text, Bill Norman, 1989

ISBN: 0 85206 981 2

Printed by Smiths of Bradford.

Introduction

FOR the last five years I have been researching aspects of the history of Teesside and Cleveland during the Second World War. In 1984 I appealed to readers of the Middlesbrough *Evening Gazette* for eye-witness accounts of the daylight bombing raid on that town's railway station on Bank Holiday Monday, 3rd August, 1942. The result was impressive: written replies reached almost 100 and there were sufficient telephone calls on the night that the appeal was issued to keep me busy for nearly six hours.

Many respondents who could provide only part of the story took the opportunity to ask for fuller details of what had happened on that day many years before, while others did not restrict their accounts to the events of 3rd August, 1942: they mentioned other incidents too, some of which I was aware; others of which I was not. Curiosity was aroused and the investigation widened. The results of my researches to date have been incorporated in one volume, *Luftwaffe over Cleveland*, which is due to be published in the near future, although extracts have already appeared in the local Press and in the aviation magazine *FlyPast*. They appear to have been well received.

During the course of my investigations I have acquired a large number of photographs of incidents and events that occurred in the area during the 1939-45 period. A number are from institutional sources but most have been borrowed from the family albums of respondents who were kind enough to share them with me. This selection is offered in the hope that it will provide an interesting glimpse into those dangerous – and occasionally exciting – times when ordinary people were often called upon to do extraordinary things.

Thanks are extended to those who generously loaned the photographs.

BOMBED, SAFE —THEN SUNK
North-East Trawlers Machine-Gunned

THE bombing of North-East trawlers and machine-gunning of their crews by Nazi raiders is graphically described by the seamen heroes to-day.

Three lifeboats, linked by ropes, have swept the seas off the East Coast in a vain bid to trace an aircraft reported down.

To-day's German communique repeats fantastic opened fire on the Active. Altogether 15 bombs were dropped, and one landed under the side of the Active...

MIDDLESBROUGH
"Salute The Soldier" Week
TOTAL: £1,100,000
a "good kick in the pants"

REGAL Stockton Tel. 66737

MONDAY, MAY 20th, 1940
ALL THE WEEK

BAND WAGGON

Featuring
ARTHUR BIG HEARTED ASKEY
RICHARD STINKER MURDOCH
— JACK HYLTON AND HIS BOYS

At :— 2.17, 4.32, 6.47, 9.2

Smoke Defended Tees-side

As a vulnerable area to enemy air attack during the war, Tees-side knows the value of the protection afforded both to industry and to the tens of thousands of people living on both banks of the river by the barrage balloon system. It can now be revealed how another defence—the smoke screen—on the home front operated and worked successfully.

Householders in the congested parts of Middlesbrough

'Phoney' Town In Cleveland Hills

CROUCHED in their tiny shelters, Tees-siders must often have wondered how the German bombers droning ahead, particularly in the Summer and Autumn of 1941, could possibly have missed the vast works and plants on the river banks.

Little Air Raid Damage On Tees-side

September, 1938. The construction of trench shelters gets underway at the Marsh Road recreation ground, Middlesbrough *(above)*, while Corporation workmen *(right)* begin work on similar projects on Clairville Common, near to the junction of Marton Road and the Longlands.

Developments in aviation during the 1920s/1930s had ensured that in any future conflict every citizen would be a potential target. As early as June 1937 the government was sufficiently alarmed by the international situation to inform local authorities of the importance of making the necessary arrangements to provide for the safety of the civilian population in the event of war breaking out. Middlesbrough's Air Raids Precautions Committee ultimately provided communal shelters for some 80 per cent of the town's population (c.100,000 places), the programme being started in September 1938, when the Munich Crisis gave particular impetus. *(Cleveland County Libraries)*

WILL'S CIGARETTES

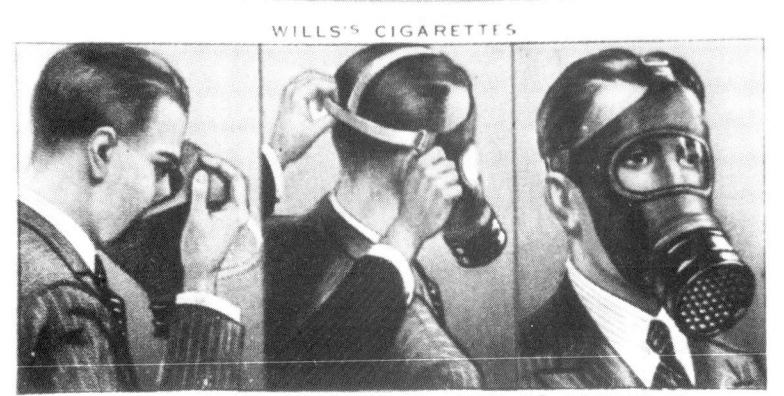

THE CIVILIAN RESPIRATOR—HOW TO ADJUST IT

Fear of gas attacks by enemy aircraft prompted the government to issue some 38 million gas masks at the time of the Munich Crisis, in September 1938. In Middlesbrough, 100,000 respirators were assembled and distributed within the space of five days by voluntary labour. Distribution of the town's gas mask cartons began in late February 1939. In the days before the "balloon went up" the Bobby on the Beat was made responsible for the distribution of the buff-coloured containers. Distribution usually took place at the blue-painted police-boxes which were dotted around the town. The picture *(above)* shows Middlesbrough PC 140 George Gibson performing his duties at the police-box which used to be sited on the corner of Southfield Road and Woodlands Road, close to the Education Offices. The recipients are ARP wardens, whose job it was to deliver the cartons to households. In addition to distribution, the volunteers carried out an important census: after ensuring that the respirators fitted properly and that the right sizes had been allocated, they compiled details of surplus masks in any household or noted the need for more. *(Mrs J. Thornton)*

In this undated photograph, Middlesbrough air raid wardens march through the town under the watchful eye of police-inspector Robert ("Bob") Stewart. Inspector Stewart had been involved with the embrionic Air Raid Precautions Service for some time before the Police ARP Department was formed in February 1939. That department was responsible for the organisation of the Special Constabulary, the Police War Reserve, Air Raid Wardens and the Messenger Services. In March 1939, he was appointed Staff Officer to the Wardens' Service and ultimately had in his charge the responsibility for 55 Wardens' Posts and over 1,000 Wardens, in addition to 21,000 Firewatchers who had been organised into 1,024 street fire parties. *(P. Stewart)*

1939 was a time for marching. Here we see Great Ayton's fire-auxiliaries parading through the village, with members of the British Legion bringing up the rear. Maurice Heavisides leads, followed by (left to right) Wilf Bickerton, Billy Teasdale and George Hoggart. *(M. Heavisides)*

In 1942 the Ayton firemen were issued with new uniforms and they used that opportunity to pose for the following group photograph – in a most unusual setting! Front: (left to right): unknown, Billy Teasdale, Fred Gibson; Middle: Maurice Heavisides, George Smith, Walter Fletcher, Ernie Burdon; Back: Kit Johnson, unknown, Billy Haigh. *(M. Heavisides)*

During the 1939–45 period most commercial vehicle production went to the armed forces, with only a limited number of small- to medium-capacity vehicles being made available to the Fire Service and to Civil Defence authorities. Perhaps in anticipation of the likely shortage of fire-fighting appliances in the event of war, the Home Office had distributed trailer pumps to brigades prior to the conflict and these could be pulled by *any* vehicle to which towing equipment had been fitted. Many large cars were thus adapted for use as emergency fire-fighting units. Other larger, private cars with long wheelbase also had the body removed from a point just behind the front doors, and ambulance bodies fitted. The men of the Great Ayton fire crew had a Ford V8 towing unit: a saloon car chassis with the rear of the body removed and a van body fabricated to carry the crew on two longitudinal seats. Two ladders were carried on the roof and small items of equipment were stowed within the body. The picture shows some of the Ayton fire-fighters practising their skills under the leadership of Maurice Heavisides (first left) in the hills behind the village, c.1942. *(M. Heavisides)*

Bob Stewart points out Middlesbrough landmarks to air raid wardens and firewatchers from the roof of the *Evening Gazette* buildings in Borough Road. *(P. Stewart)*

Autumn, 1939. A Thornaby-based Avro Anson of 220 Squadron (Coastal Command) on patrol over a North East convoy. In September 1939 Thornaby aerodrome was transferred from Bomber Command to Coastal Command. That same month, 220 Squadron arrived with their Ansons but almost immediately began to re-equip with Lockheed Hudsons. It was a Hudson from this squadron that crashed into houses in Cambridge Road, Middlesbrough, on 8th November, 1939, after an engine failed while the pilot was making a landing approach to Thornaby. The four occupants of the aircraft were killed. In February 1940, three Hudsons from Thornaby located the German prison ship *Altmark* in a Norwegian fjord and the Royal Navy was able to intercept and release 299 British prisoners of war. *(Author's collection)*

RAF fitters overhaul a Lockheed Hudson at Thornaby aerodrome, c.1940. *(Author's collection)*

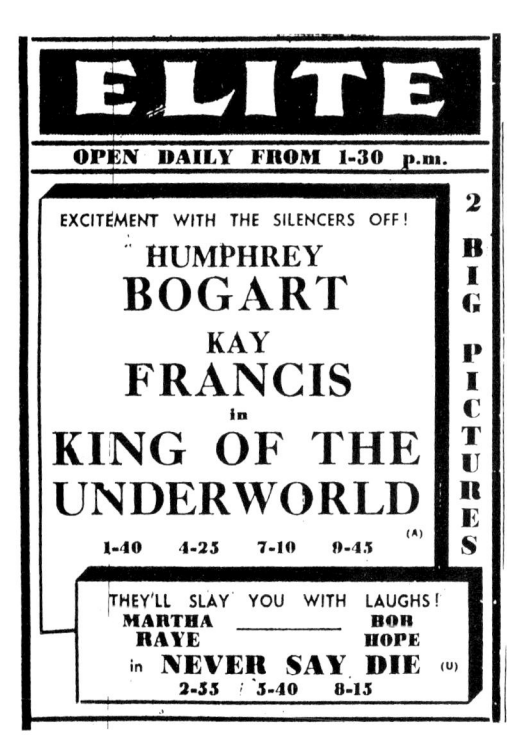

ENTERTAINMENTS PAGE

ELITE
OPEN DAILY FROM 1-30 p.m.

2 BIG PICTURES

EXCITEMENT WITH THE SILENCERS OFF!

HUMPHREY **BOGART**
KAY **FRANCIS**
in
KING OF THE UNDERWORLD

1-40   4-25   7-10   9-45 (A)

THEY'LL SLAY YOU WITH LAUGHS!

MARTHA **RAYE** — BOB **HOPE**
in **NEVER SAY DIE** (U)

2-35   5-40   8-15

REGENT PALLADIUM
MIDDLESBROUGH

MONDAY, TUESDAY, WEDNESDAY:
THE RITZ BROS. in
THE GOLDWYN FOLLIES (U)
with EDGAR BERGEN and CHARLIE McCARTHY
In Glorious Technicolor.

THURSDAY, FRIDAY, SATURDAY:
MICKEY ROONEY in
The Adventures of HUCKLEBERRY FINN (U)
with WALTER CONNOLLY.

MIDDLESBROUGH
6.30—Twice Nightly—8.40
MON., TUES., WED. NEXT
EMLYN WILLIAMS and ANNA KONSTAM in
THEY DRIVE BY NIGHT (A)

THURS., FRI. & SAT. NEXT
Mischa Auer, Mary Boland, Edward Everett Horton in
LITTLE TOUGH GUYS IN SOCIETY (U)
All Seats Bookable. 'Phone 8513.

REGENT · REDCAR

TO-MORROW (SUNDAY), at 8 p.m. PRICES: 2/-, 1/6, 1/-. NO BOOKING FEE.

RADIO'S ACE VOCALIST AND REDCAR'S MOST POPULAR STAR
MONTE REY
Singing the Popular Songs of Three Years. Don't Miss Him.

OWEN WALTERS and his FULL ORCHESTRA of 12 Performers
with Don Wilson—Leslie Pront—Al Davis—Ellen Bartley.

SEPTEMBER 4th.—Three Days Only—Wallace Beery, Laraine Day in SERGEANT MADDEN.
SEPTEMBER 7th.—Victor McLaglen, Chester Morris, Wendy Barrie in PACIFIC LINER.

THE PLAZA, Stockton   6.6—Continuous—10.48
MONDAY NEXT.
ANNA STEN and ALAN MARSHALL in
EXILE EXPRESS
A beautiful alien exiled from a land she has learned to love.
With WALTER CATLETT and JED PROUTY.
Also Leon Ames and Jean Woodbury in CIPHER BUREAU.
Thursday:—TRANSATLANTIC MERRY-GO-ROUND.

REGAL Stockton
Tel. 66737.

MONDAY, September 4, 1939
ALL THE WEEK

Basil **Rathbone**
Boris **Karloff**
in
SON OF FRANKENSTEIN

At:— 3.20   6.15   9.9

Also

GLENDA FARRELL in **EXPOSED**

At:— 2.8   5.3   7.58

SCALA

Continuous Daily from 1.30 p.m. For Six Days.

GEORGE ARLISS & CESAR ROMERO
in **CARDINAL RICHLIEU**
Showing at 3.10—6.15—9.20 p.m. (U)

Also

KAY FRANCIS & RONALD COLMAN
in **CYNARA**
Showing at 1.35—4.40—7.45 p.m. (A)

TO-DAY — GHOST GOES WEST AND COME AND GET IT

ODEON MIDDLESBROUGH

CAR PARK — Phone 2888

WEEK COMMENCING SEPTEMBER 4th
NOTE.—MATINEE DAILY 2.15 p.m. EVENINGS CONTINUOUS FROM 6 p.m. SATURDAY, 2 BOOKABLE HOUSES, 6 и 8.30 p.m.

ENCORE!

THREE LITTLE MAIDS — 1929 — WE GAVE YOU TALKIES
1939 — WE GIVE YOU ENCORES

TIT WILLOW

GILBERT and SULLIVAN'S **The MIKADO**

IN COLOUR SUCH AS YOU NEVER SAW BEFORE
THE MUSIC—THE SONGS—YOU ALL KNOW

THE FLOWERS THAT BLOOM IN THE SPRING

WANDERING MINSTREL

BEHOLD THE LORD HIGH EXECUTIONER

HEAR THEM — APPLAUD THEM — HEAR THEM AGAIN

I AM SO PROUD

ENCORES — THE SCREENS GREATEST INNOVATION

Showing AFTERNOONS 2.15. EVENINGS 6.35 and 8.45.

GLOBE

AN A.B.C. THEATRE.

MICKEY ROONEY
in MARK TWAIN'S
THE ADVENTURES OF Huckleberry Finn (U)

WITH
WALTER CONNOLLY
WILLIAM FRAWLEY • REX INGRAM
3-10   6-15   9-15

— ALSO —

The Lady and The Mob
WITH
FAY BAINTER • IDA LUPINO • WARREN HYMER (U)
2-0   5-0   8-0

GAUMONT MIDDLESBROUGH

IN TECHNICOLOR
THE LITTLE PRINCESS (U)
featuring
SHIRLEY TEMPLE
RICHARD GREENE
ANITA LOUISE
3.20—6.15—9.0.

"The Jones Family
EVERYBODY'S BABY"
2.10—5.0—7.50.

HIPPODROME MIDDLESBROUGH

Continuous from 2.0 p.m.
WALTER PIDGEON
VIRGINIA BRUCE
Leo Carillo in
SOCIETY LAWYER (A)
Showing at 3.35—6.30—9.25 p.m.

TOMMY RYAN in
ORPHANS OF THE STREET (U)
Showing at 2.20, 5.15, 8.10 p.m.

See Events of the World through the New Series "March of Time."

PAVILION MIDDLESBROUGH

MONDAY
ALICE FAYE, CONSTANCE BENNETT in
TAIL SPIN (A)
6.45 p.m. and 9.35 p.m.

THURSDAY
FRITZ KORTNER, WYNNE GIBSON in
THE CROUCHING BEAST
6.50 p.m. and 9.35 p.m. (A)

North-Eastern Gazette

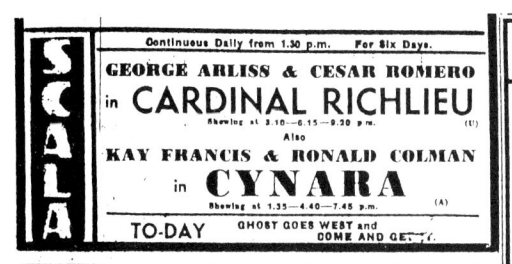

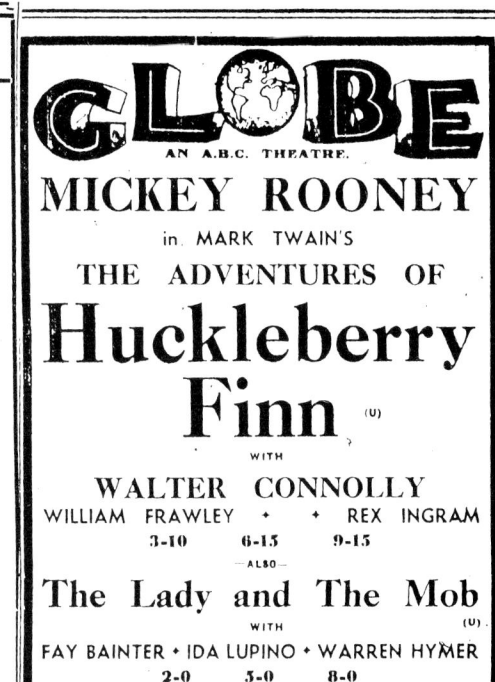

SPECIAL

THE ONLY EVENING PAPER PUBLISHED IN TEES-SIDE AND DISTRICT.

TEL. 2451.   MIDDLESBROUGH, SATURDAY, SEPTEMBER 2, 1939.   BROADCASTING: PAGE 3

EMPIRE STOCKTON

MON., TUES., WED.
CONRAD VEIDT
JILL ESMOND
LESLIE FENTON
in
SECRETS OF F.P.1 (U)
3.30, 6.25, 9.20.
ALSO
GENE AUTREY, SMILEY BURNETTE in
PRAIRIE MOON
2.10, 5.5, 8.0.

THURS., FRI., SAT.
ALEXANDER GRAY
VIVIENNE SEGAL
WALTER PIDGEON
in
VIENNESE NIGHTS (U)
In Technicolor 3.0—5.30—8.55.
ALSO
BARRY K. BARNES, GOOGIE WITHERS in
YOU'RE THE DOCTOR
4.0, 7.25.

Entertainments in Middlesbrough the week war was declared.

On the afternoon of 17th October, 1939, three Spitfires of 41 Squadron, Catterick, shot down a Heinkel 111 which was en-route to the Firth of Forth on a reconnaisance mission to locate the battle-crusier HMS *Hood*. The Heinkel "ditched" in the sea some 25 miles east of Whitby: two of its crew of four were already dead when the aircraft hit the water. The two survivors, Unteroffiziers Bernhard Hochstuhl (radio-operator) and Eugen Lange (pilot), managed to scramble into a small rubber dinghy seconds before the aircraft sank, taking with it the food and drink they had hoped would sustain them until eventual rescue.

The survivors spent two precarious nights at sea – bitterly cold, without sleep and all the time paddling with their hands to keep their craft head-on to the rough sea – before a current caught their boat and finally carried it to the foot of the cliffs one mile north of Sandsend station. By then, Lange was suffering from exposure and nearly unconscious and it was left to Hochstuhl, who was near to exhaustion, to scale the cliff in search of help. He was arrested close to the entrance to Sandsend tunnel by George Thomas, an LNER Special Constable, who escorted him to the railway station before organising Lange's rescue.

Lange's rescue was effected by George Thomas, Jack Barker (the Lythe duty constable) and Frank Dring, a Sandsend painter. Using the deflated dinghy as a stretcher, and with Frank Dring *underneath* it to prevent the dinghy from swaying so much that it might imbalance them and send them all crashing below, they pulled, clawed – and occasionally crawled – their way to the top. It was a *very* difficult climb.

After a short stay in Whitby Hospital, Lange and Hochstuhl, *the first Germans to be captured on English soil during World War II,* were transferred to London for interrogation before being shipped to Canada, where they spent the rest of the war.

In 1979, Bernhard Hochstuhl and Eugen Lange revisited Sandsend and Whitby on the 40th anniversary of their rescue, when they were reunited with their rescuers and those who had nursed them back to health. The only person not present was George Thomas: he had died six months earlier. His son took his place.

Above: October, 1939. Bernhard Hochstuhl is carried from Whitby Hospital to a waiting car and to ultimate internment until the cessation of hostilities. *(Author's collection)*

Left: Forty years after: Eugen Lange (left) and Bernhard Hochstuhl revisit the site of their rescue on 19th October, 1939. *(Whitby Gazette)*

Immediately prior to the war British scientists had hurriedly prepared for service a chain of rudimentary radar stations which, by the summer of 1939, was able to detect aircraft approaching at medium or high level at distances of some 100 miles; these stations were Fighter Command's long-range "eyes". When war was declared there were 18 of these radar stations, code-named Chain Home (CH), in operation and giving interlocking cover along the eastern and southern coasts of Britain between Portsmouth and Aberdeen. The term "radar" (RAdio Detection And Ranging) was not coined until after the Americans entered the war in 1941: prior to that time the system was referred to as RDF (Radio Direction Finding).

There were two CH stations in Yorkshire: one at Staxton Wold, Scarborough, and the other at Danby Beacon. Although the above photograph of the Danby site was taken in the early 1950s, the only perceivable difference from war-time days is the replaced sign-post which had been removed at the outbreak of war. There can be little doubt, as the *Yorkshire Evening News* was to point out in September, 1945, "...that but for Danby station, Yorkshire would have suffered far worse raids than it did. The WAAFs on this station, many of whom were from West Riding homes, kept track of every hostile plane and enabled fighters to head them off".

Danby's first success came on 3rd February, 1940, when Hurricanes of 43 Squadron, Acklington, were alerted and successfully intercepted a German raider, which was subsequently shot down near Whitby. The station was officially closed down on 30th November, 1945, but it was not until the 1950s that the buildings and the 360 feet-high towers were levelled. *(F. Smith)*

The Operations Block, Danby Beacon, 1945. *(via F. Smith)*

There were 13 observation posts in the Teesside/Cleveland area: their aim was to ensure the accurate identification of aircraft – both friendly and hostile – overflying specified areas. The posts were sited at Eaglescliffe, Eston, Redcar, Seaton Carew, West Hartlepool, Loftus, Hinderwell, Castleton, Ayton, Newton Bewley and Saltburn, the latter perhaps gaining more experience than the rest because of the fact that raiders aiming for Teesside tended to cross the coast at Huntcliffe.

Posts were usually located in elevated spots off the beaten track and initially consisted of little more than a circle of layered sandbags with an inner circle of corrugated iron: in the early days a spluttering oil stove and the sandbags were the only protection against inclement weather. Each post was manned by two men at all times – each pair completing a "watch" of four hours. All were volunteers, though some were full-timers and others worked part-time, and were drawn from a variety of occupations. Each received 1s 3d per hour, the full-timers working a 48-hour week.

When an aircraft was detected by sight or by sound its height and direction of flight were determined and its position "fixed" on a plotting table. The information was then passed to all other posts in the neighbourhood. Once an incoming aircraft crossed

A two-man crew on duty at the plotting table of the Eaglescliffe Royal Observer Corps post, 1945. *(Author's collection)*

the coast its position was passed from post to post so that the aircraft was never "lost". Details were also transmitted to the regional Fighter Command HQ for appropriate action.

The Redcar post had a "special" observer among its personnel: "Paddy", a smooth-haired fox-terrier belonging to the WR Vincent, the head observer, developed an uncanny accuracy in detecting approaching hostile aircraft. The dog would prick up its ears when a faint drone was heard and would listen intently for a moment. Then in would settle down or "walk about in a bustling sort of way". Whenever the dog "bustled", the drone usually came from a raider.

The photograph (left) shows members of the 03/9 Royal Observer Corps Unit, Hinderwell, in June 1945. Those pictured are (left to right) *Back row:* Mr Goldstraw, Leo Welford, Tom Jefferson, Ronnie Toes, Bill Welford, Alan Grainger, Bill White and Mr Wilks; *Middle row:* George Foster, Joe Dawson, George Sherwood, Gibson Jefferson and Harry Heseltine; *Front row:* Herman Wood, Reg Barrett, Captain Codling, Harold Featherstone, Percy Tawn, Willie Harrison and Bob Sanderson. *(Ms T. Wilkinson)*

3rd February, 1940. The wreck of a Heinkel 111 (1H+FM) of 4.II/KG26 ("Lowen Geschwader") lies in a field close to the cottages of Bannial Flatt Farm, some two miles north of Whitby. This was the first German aircraft to crash on English soil during the last war. It was shot down by three Hurricanes of 43 Squadron (based at Acklington, Northumberland) after it had attacked a trawler some three miles off Whitby. One of the pilots responsible was Peter Townsend (later, Group Captain and Equerry to Queen Elizabeth II), who became famous during the 1950s because of his love for Princess Margaret. *(E. Baxter/Evening Gazette)*

When the Minister of Agriculture coined the phrase "Dig for Victory" on 4th October, 1939, he was addressing not only farmers but also everyone who had a garden. The ultimate aim was to make Britain self-sufficient in food and to that end arable farming was extended at the expense of pastoral, and householders increased their output by turning lawns and flower-beds over to vegetables. All spare land in towns was also utilised, including the patch adjacent to the Cenotaph outside Albert Park gates. In this picture, taken in April 1940, a group of boys from Ayresome Senior School prepare land for potato planting. The car showroom in the background (left) still stands, but nowadays it sells Japanese cars. The ground so enthusiastically tilled by the six boys now forms one of the flower-beds which surround the Cenotaph. *(E. Baxter/Evening Gazette)*

DIG FOR VICTORY

is now a National Slogan, but you must also have the BEST SEEDS to get the BEST RESULTS—and that means

FEWSTERS

STOCKTON and THORNABY

Tel. 6452   Est. 101 Years

20,000 TOMATO PLANTS NOW READY IN VARIETY

SCOTCH SEED POTATOES

VARIETIES IN STOCK.

ARRAN COMRADE
BRITISH QUEEN
DARGILL EARLY
DUKE OF YORK
ECLIPSE. EPICURE
GREAT SCOT
KING EDWARD
MAY QUEEN
MIDLOTHIAN EARLY
SHARPE'S EXPRESS
ARRAN PILOT
ARRAN BANNER
ARRAN CHIEF
KERR'S PINK
DOON STAR
MAJESTIC
RED KING

1940. The retained fire crew of Stokesley's Fire Brigade pose alongside their Morris Commercial appliance in T. Durham's farmyard, where the machine was kept. *Front row* (left to right): J. Jackson, J. Coulson, W. King, G. Dobson, C. Smith, R. Walshaw, J. Durham, T. Durham, G. Hallworth, L. Armstrong, R. Chapman and C. Moon. *Back row:* A. Johnson, R. Borthwick, P. Leng, S. Swales, B. Armstrong, W. Kearsley, N. Percival and J. Lilystone. *(G. Perkins)*

1940. Stokesley retained fireman, J. Coulson, stands with extinguisher at the ready as he poses alongside the Brigade's Morris Commercial appliance. Note the hooded headlight, a condition imposed by the Blackout Regulations for all vehicles. The purpose of such devices was to ensure that the feeble light that was allowed to illuminate a vehicle's nocturnal progress was not spotted by enemy aircraft. *(G. Perkins)*

Whenever residents of the Billingham Urban District Council area had to be transported to hospital during the Second World War it tended to be done in style – in the back of the Rolls Royce shown here, the tail-gate being lowered in order to accommodate stretcher and patient. Although it was not unusual for authorities to commandeer private vehicles for emergency services during the war, the Rolls Royce did not come into that category. In the Billingham UDC area it was the Fire Brigade who had staffed the ambulance service before the war and they continued to do so during the conflict. The Rolls had been in regular use by the Brigade long before the deterioration of the international situation and, indeed, it continued to be so after the German surrender and until the introduction of the National Health Service. In the picture above, Billingham firemen pose with their pride and joy; right, a young patient is loaded on board. *(J.P. Richmond)*

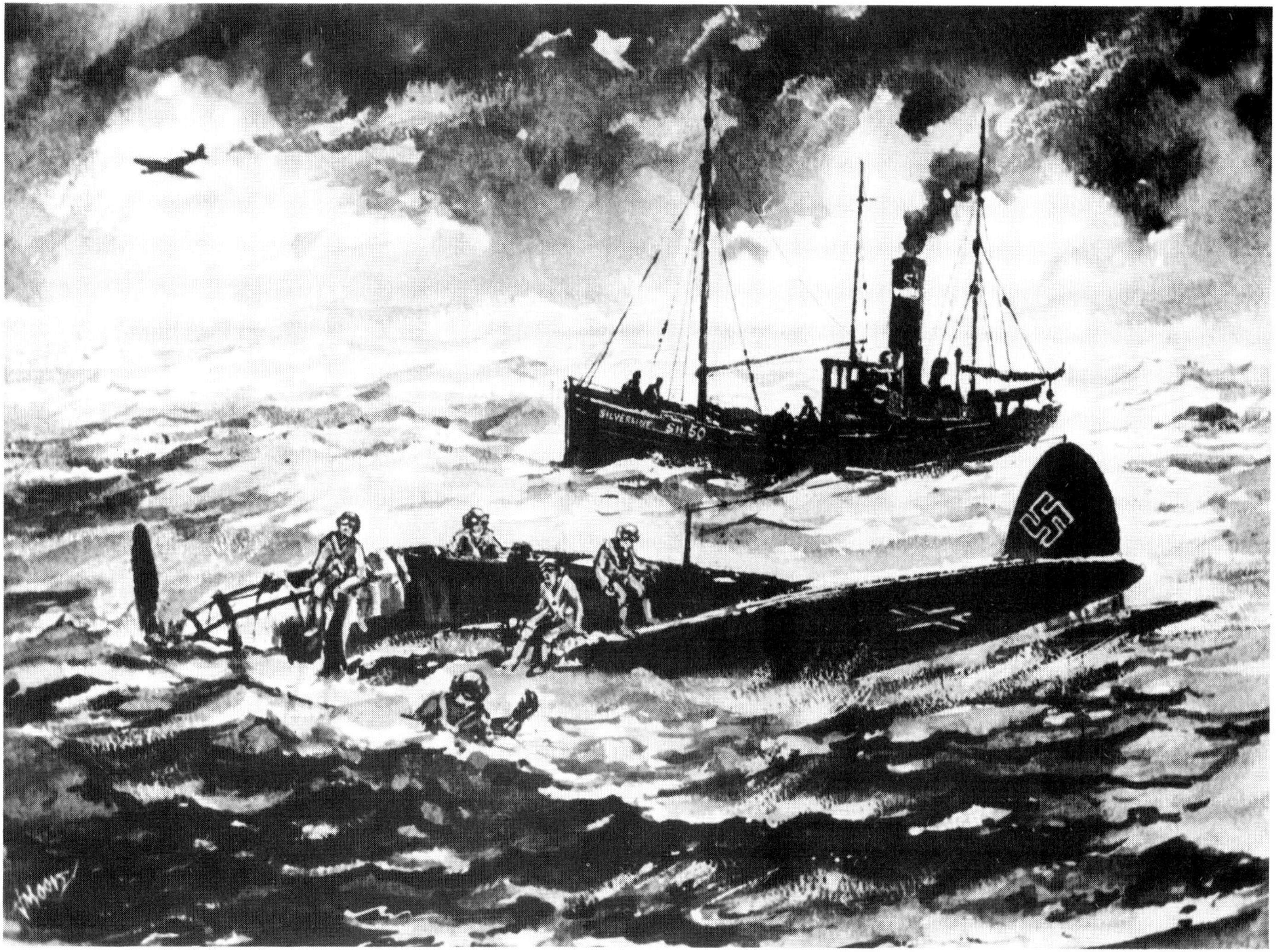

Opposite: On 3rd April, 1940, a Spitfire of 41 Squadron, RAF, entered the history books when it became the first fighter aircraft to be lost to the Luftwaffe in defence of these shores during the Second World War. The fighter, flown by Flt/Lt. Norman Ryder, had left Greatham airfield (RAF West Hartlepool), where it was on daily detachment from Catterick aeordrome, to intercept a Heinkel 111 (1H+AC) of II/KG26 which was harrassing shipping off the North Yorkshire coast. In the ensuing combat the adversaries shot each other down: the German crew were rescued by the Scarborough trawler *Silver Line* and were landed at Scarborough; Ryder was picked up by the Grimsby trawler *Alaskan* after ditching in rough seas some 15 miles east of Redcar and was subsequently landed at Hartlepool. On 25th March, 1941, *Alaskan* struck a mine off Easington, County Durham, and sank: it is not known how its crew fared. The picture shows an artist's impression (by John Moore) of *Silver Line* drawing alongside the stricken Heinkel while Ryder's damaged Spitfire endeavours to reach the coast. *(Author's collection)*

Top, right: The Scarborough drifter, *Silver Line* (left). *(G. Scales)*

Bottom, right: Some of the crew of *Silver Line* pose with one of the statuettes of a lifeboatman which every member received from the then Mayor of Scarborough in recognition of the part each played in the rescue. The mementos were a gift from the Scarborough Corporation and were presented at a Civic Reception at the Town Hall on 6th April, 1940. Left to right: Chas. Hunter (gun-loader); Ted Robinson; Bill Watkinson (skipper); Tom Watkinson (gunner); Bob Watkinson (mate). Other members of the crew were: A. Barley (engineer); W.G. Cole (2nd engineer); and D. Holmes (cook). Forty-eight years later, Bill Watkinson's grandson also had a brush with the Luftwaffe when, as skipper of a much more modern *Silver Line*, he netted a ten-foot German landmine off Flamborough! *(P. Watkinson)*

In mid-May 1940, as the German advance through France continued and fears of invasion grew, Anthony Eden (Secretary of State for War) broadcast to the men of Britain to form units of Local Defence Volunteers (LDV). The appeal offered an opportunity to those who, because of age or work, could not join the Services but who wanted to "hit back". Thus within 24 hours, 250,000 men had answered the call and that number had grown to 1,000,000 by 23rd July when, at Churchill's suggestion, the LDV was renamed Home Guard. Middlesbrough formed two battallions, the 37th and the 60th. On 25th January, 1941, they became the 8th and 9th North Riding (Middlesbrough) Battallions, respectively, and Green Howards badges were distributed.

Participation was voluntary. It was also unpaid, but a uniform and a rifle were provided free of charge. Provision of the latter often took some time: when George Coupland (Dormanstown) joined at Warrenby works in 1940 he had to go on patrol of the works armed only with a stick! Later, he was provided with a 12-bore shot-gun – without ammunition – and used to rattle the bolt to scare those people he had to challenge during the hours of darkness.

Each large industrial unit had its own defence contingent, drawn from employees; their task was to guard that unit during the hours of darkness – and often after a day's work – while the danger of invasion existed. As that threat receded, many Home Guard units trained for local Anti-Aircraft defence. The Middlesbrough contingents first manned the ack-ack defences on the night of 6th/7th July, 1942, when the town suffered an incendiary attack. The last parade of local Home Guard units took place on 4th December, 1944, when it was noted that 23,000 officers and men had served in the Tees Garrison, including 3,500 who had served continuously since volunteering in 1940. The photograph above shows the HQ Company, 8th Battallion Green Howards (Home Guard) whose base was the Drill Hall, Bright Street, Middlesbrough. *(G. Perkins)*

MISS JEAN BATTEN

On Friday, 24th May, 1940, a fleet of six ambulances belonging to the Anglo-French Ambulance Corps called at Middlesbrough and Stockton. The vehicles, which had been presented to the Corps by the Durham Mineworkers' Federation at cost of £500 each for service in France, were en-route to Durham in the charge of Corps Adjutant B.T. Slinn. In Durham they would be formally handed over to the Corps by David Grenfell, MP. When the Mayor of Middlesbrough (Cllr Sir William Crosthwaite) inspected the fleet he met Miss Jean Batten (a famous airwoman who had achieved fame with her record-breaking Australia–England flights during the 1930s), who had recently joined the Corps. The photograph (left) shows a group at the inspection and includes the Mayor, Miss Batten (on the Mayor's right), Capt. Slinn, Ald. S.A. Sadler and Cllr H. French (left). During her visit, Miss Batten confessed that she found ambulance driving rather unexciting but that she expected that it would become pretty lively when the group reached France. In the light of subsequent events, perhaps it became too lively!

In May, 1940, the Corps had a unit of 22 fully equipped ambulances in France and another 22 almost ready for shipment. It was hoped that other vehicles on order would soon bring the total strength to 110 vehicles in a very short time: over 50 towns in the country had undertaken to provide and equip vehicles. Following the visit, the Mayor decided to present a fully-equipped vehicle in the name of the town to the Corps, while in Stockton the Mayor and Mayoress, Alderman and Mrs J.W. Gargate, instigated a fund to do the same. *(E. Baxter/Evening Gazette)*

On the evening of Friday, 24th May, 1940, Teddy Joyce and his Band took a break from their engagement at the Middlesbrough Empire to play at Redcar's Pier Ballroom, where some patrons took time off from their dancing to pose for this group photograph. Hours after this picture was taken, the musicians – and possibly some of those shown above – were passing through South Bank when they were caught up in Teesside's first air raid, in the early hours of Saturday, 25th May. The attack resulted in eight civilian casualties – the first time that civilians had been injured in a bombing raid on England. A number of motorists returning home from the dance stopped their cars and dived into ditches when they heard the bombs whistling down; the band's coach suffered broken windows while crossing the railway bridge near the tramway depot when a bomb narrowly missed the bridge and exploded in a field alongside it. The man wearing the bow tie (extreme left) is Jim Cox, of Redcar, who was to have a narrow escape of his own during the daylight raid on Middlesbrough railway station two years later. *(J. Cox)*

EMPIRE MIDDLESBROUGH
6-30 – 'PHONE 2346 – 8-30

COMMENCING MONDAY, 20th MAY, FOR SIX DAYS.

Welcome Reappearance of the Universally Popular Radio Personality—

TEDDY JOYCE
AND HIS BAND
with

LORNA MARTIN
England's Champion Accordionist.

BABS DUDLEY
The New Singing Sensation.

DUNCAN WHITE
Britain's Hottest Trumpeter.

BILLY GUEST — Electric Guitarist

AND AN ENTIRELY NEW ALL-COMEDY PROGRAMME.
THIRTY FIRST-CLASS STARS IN A WHIRLWIND OF
MELODY, COMEDY, DANCING and THRILLS GALORE

Box Office Open 11 till 4 and 5.45 to 7.45. : Please Bring Your Gas Mask

May, 1940. The presentation of the first war-time ambulance to the town of Redcar takes place outside the municipal buildings, Coatham Road. Numbering from left to right, the party includes: Ald. C. Harris (fourth), Mayor J. Coupland (tenth), *then* Cllr J.T. Fletcher, Dr E. Fallows, Mr H. Caldwell (Town Clerk), Mr and Mrs J.T. Welford and Cllr Mrs I. Lonsdale. Note the headlight hoods, fitted to comply with the Blackout Regulations. *(Kirkleatham Museum)*

In the summer of 1940 the strong belief that the invasion of this country was imminent prompted the authorities to take measures which they hoped might hinder the progress of an enemy. Direction and other road signs were removed and road barriers were set up throughout the area (and the nation); concrete pill-boxes were constructed at strategic points and large blocks of concrete set down as tank traps at any location considered to be vulnerable. On the coast, Cleveland's beaches were littered with concrete blocks and steel spikes to obstruct the movement of enemy vehicles that might manage to negotiate the landmines set just below the surface of the sand; at both Saltburn and Redcar the military authorities closed the piers to general use and dismantled parts of them to prevent their possible use by an invader; barbed wire stretched from the Teesmouth to Saltburn; and between Marske and Redcar the Stray saw an accumulation of pill-boxes, machine-gun posts and searchlight emplacements while in the rugby field close to Green Lane the guns of an ack-ack battery pointed skywards.

This undated war-time picture of Redcar promenade has a depressive air about it: the sand-bags, the shuttered amusement palaces and cafes, and the barbed-wire all combine to give the resort a grim countenance. *(Cleveland County Libraries)*

Films on offer, week commencing 9th September, 1940. Considering this country's predicament in 1940, one cannot help but feel that the film on show at Stockton's *Empire* cinema was much more the truth than that being offered at the *Globe*.

On 10th June, 1940, Mussolini declared war in Germany's favour. Within minutes of the announcement, Middlesbrough police – following Home Office directives – began to round-up Italian aliens in the borough. In the evening of the declaration a hostile crowd of demonstrators toured the streets and attacked six well-known Italian-owned ice-cream saloons and cafes. In Linthorpe Road, Grange Road, Suffield Street, Newport Road and Corporation Road large stones were hurled through plate-glass windows and at shop fronts. The police took 28 Italian residents between the ages of 16 and 70 into protective custody and reinforcements of police were stationed in large numbers in the vicinity of establishments bearing Italian names. A number of demonstrators were subsequently taken into custody. On 11th June, police picketed several Italian-owned establishments which had been damaged the night before. One of those was Costantino's, which stood in Newport Road, opposite Newport Crescent and the current Binns store, on the site now occupied by Dunn and Co. *(E. Baxter/ Evening Gazette)*

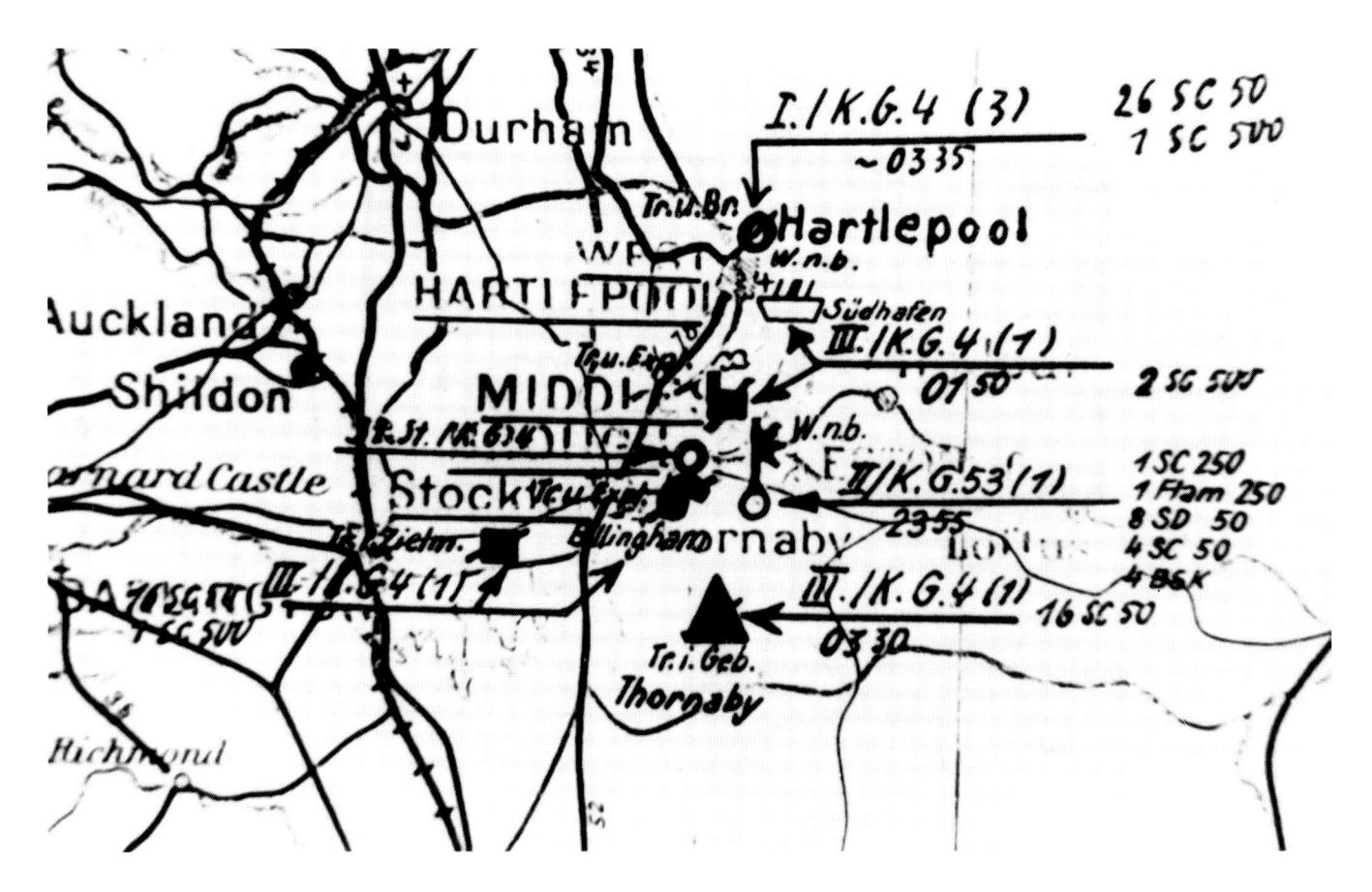

The Luftwaffe prepared a detailed operations map for every raid on Britain. The picture shows targets, bomb loads, units involved and times of attack of a relay of raids on Teesside on the night of 24th/25th August, 1940. For example, I/KG4 was the unit detailed to attack Hartlepool with three aircraft at 0335hrs on 25th August; in total those aircraft were detailed to drop 26 bombs of 50 kilogrammes each and one bomb of 500 kilogrammes.

Not all of the aircraft that participated in the raid were of the same type, nor were they based at the same airfield. I/KG4 flew Heinkel 111s from Soesterberg; III/KG4 flew Junkers 88s from Amsterdam/Schipol; and II/KG53 flew Heinkel 111s from Lille.

Some specific targets can be identified. For example, the attack at 0150 was aimed at the Tees Power station and, probably, Smith's Dock (Südhafen); the 0330 raid had Thornaby aerodrome as its target. Unfortunately, the other symbols remain a mystery.

The available records indicate that the 0150 raid on Middlesbrough commenced five minutes early; that a total of 14 HE (some of which were unexploded) fell in the County Borough; and that none of the designated targets was hit. There was one fatality: a nine-year-old girl in Grangetown. *(Bundesarchiv)*

Nur für den Dienstgebrauch **Zielstammkarte** Land: Großbritannien England (Yorkshire)	Ort: Middlesbrough (Nähere Lage) am rechten Ufer des River Tees, etwa 500 m im O des Hauptbahnhofs. Geogr. Werte: 54° 34' 35" N 1° 13' 14" W	Ziel-Nr. G.B. 45 10 mit G.B. 61 10 Kartenbl.-Nr. E 6/1:100 000 E. B. Nr. E 15/1:63 360

1. **Bezeichnung des Zieles:**
   Hafenanlagen.
   Chemische Werke "Sadler & Co. Ltd.".

   Vgl. mit Ziel-Nr. G.B. 61 1 Teerdestillationsanlage "Clarence Works", 0,9 km im NO.

2. **Bedeutung:**
   Middlesbrough ist Haupteinfuhrhafen für Eisenerze.
   Die Ausfuhr besteht aus Eisen- und Stahlwaren, Maschinen sowie Produkten der Kokerei- und chemischen Industrie.

3. **Beschreibung des Zieles:** Höhe über NN: 5 m.

   a) Verkehrsanschlüsse: Straßenverbindung. Wasseranschluß über River Tees zur Nordsee. Eigener Gleisansanschluß. Nächster Bahnhof Middlesbrough Hauptbahnhof (500 m im W).

   b) Ausdehnung insgesamt: Etwa 385 000 qm.   Bebaute Fläche: Etwa 20 000 qm.
   W-O etwa 1100 m
   N-S etwa 900 m.

Part of a German Intelligence document detailing aspects of Sadler's Chemical Works, Port Clarence, and other potential targets in the immediate vicinity. The Luftwaffe and German Intelligence had numerous maps, aerial photographs and models of the Tees area. Such aids to orientation were supplemented by documents such as that shown here which gave a complete breakdown of each building on any particular target site, to the extent that functions and dimensions were listed. Documents in the writer's possession show every potential target of industrial and commercial importance in the Tees area and each group of documents pin-point specific units and buildings within each complex: Warrenby Ironworks; Cleveland Ironworks; Cargo Fleet Works; Smith's Dockyard; Middlesbrough Docks; every plant in the Ironmasters' District; Furness Shipyards, Haverton Hill; and ICI Billingham are all shown in the greatest detail.

The Tees area was not exceptional: it simply mirrored the *national* coverage that the Germans had embarked upon before the onset of the conflict, much of the information coming from Ordnance Survey maps, post-cards, trade publications and annual accounts of industrial and economic performance which had been freely available in shops and libraries before the outbreak of war.

The German Intelligence services drew on all of these sources – and others – and sifted those which had strategic value. *(Author's collection)*

GB 6I 2 b è mit 50 39 b ♂
Nur für den Dienstgebrauch

Bild Nr. 0989/40-065 (Lfl. 2)

Aufnahme vom 14. 9. 40

Middlesbrough-Billingham
Chemisches Werk „Imperial Chem. Industries"
mit Kraftwerk „North Tees"

Länge (westl. Greenw.): 1° 16' 20''   Breite: 54° 35' 25''
Mißweisung: — 11° 34' (Mitte 1941)   Zielhöhe über NN 15 m
Maßstab etwa 1 : 15 800

Genst. 5. Abt.   Mai 1941
Karte 1 : 100 000
GB/E 6

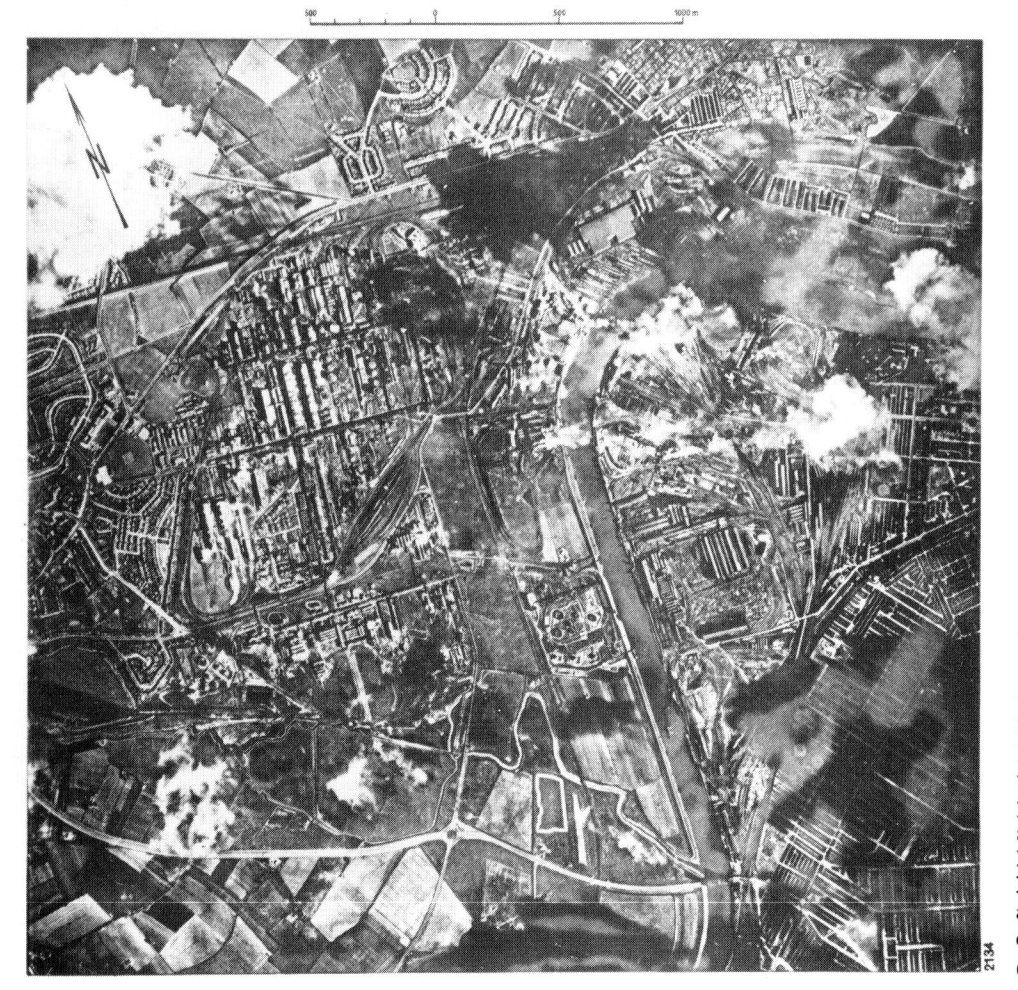

A Luftwaffe Intelligence photograph of Middlesbrough and Billingham, taken on 14th September, 1940. The picture clearly shows the Middlesbrough Ironmasters' District, south of the Tees loop, the ICI chemical plants and power station, and the Furness shipbuilding yards at Haverton Hill. The "craters" in the bottom left-hand corner are anti-aircraft gun emplacements.
(Imperial War Museum)

In Middlesbrough the principal target area for the bombs of the Luftwaffe must surely have been the Ironmasters' District, which occupied the rough triangle of land on the south side of the Tees loop and between the Newport and Transporter Bridges. Not only did that site embrace the Acklam and Britannia group of iron and steelworks of Gjers Mills and Dorman, Long but the north bank of the river provided the location for the Furness Shipyards at Haverton Hill (upper right) and the ICI chemical plant at Billingham (upper left). However, in spite of this concentration, it would seem that it was on only relatively rare occasions that such industrial targets were hit during air raids: even then, damage tended to be light. More often than not, bombs intended for the Ironmasters' District fell in open country or they fell – with tragic consequences – on the working class residential areas that fringed the southern edge of the railway from Newport to Albert Road. *(Author's collection)*

The Middlesbrough Ironmasters' District effectively masked by industrial haze. Later generations were to denounce such atmospheric pollution as being injurious to health, but during wartime there were those who believed that such emissions provided a protective screen which made accurate aerial bombing difficult and which was largely responsible for many bombs going astray and exploding in open country. Early in 1941 such "normal" emissions were supplemented by the distribution of hundreds of oil-burning furnaces – "like tar machines" – which were spaced at intervals along roadside kerbs at strategic points around the town, especially in close proximity to great industrial establishments and in and around ICI Billingham. When a raid was impending, it was the responsibility of the Pioneer Corps, acting under the Ministry of Home Security, to ignite the furnaces in particular locations, dependent upon wind direction. As they burned, the fires produced large volumes of dense black smoke to screen the town from raiders. *(Author's Collection)*

In September, 1940, Alan Deere was a Flight Lieutenant with 54 (Spitfire) Squadron. Deere served with great distinction both during the Battle of Britain and after it. In continuous action from the outbreak of the war until 1943, his official "score" was: 22 enemy aircraft destroyed; 10 probables; 18 damaged.

In September 1940, the squadron was "rested" from the Battle which was raging in the south and was posted to Catterick, where it was to operate as a temporary training unit until it returned to the south of England in February 1941. Alan Deere was much involved in the training programme – and it almost cost him his life on 28th December, 1940, when his Spitfire was in collision with that of one of his trainees (Sgt. Squires) some 10,000 feet above Crathorne, near Yarm.

Deere landed 400 yards from his aircraft at Town End farm, Kirklevington. Squires landed at Kirklevington Hall and his aircraft crashed into the banks of the River Leven at Red Hall farm. In September 1987 a team of aviation enthusiasts excavated the site of Deere's Spitfire to a depth of twenty feet to recover numerous assorted items from an aeroplane once flown by one of the most celebrated of Battle of Britain pilots.

The photograph shows Alan Deere (front row, second from left) with pilots of 54 Squadron, 1940. *(A.C. Deere)*

"For a split second I caught a glimpse of the nose of his aircraft on top of me and the next second he had flown into me. His airscrew chewed clean through my tailplane and immediately my Spitfire whipped into a vicious spin, completely out of control.

"In a matter of seconds I had jettisoned the hood and proceeded with the business of baling out having, of course, first carried out the preliminaries of releasing my cockpit straps and freeing my R/T lead. To get out of the aircraft was not going to be easy, as I soon discovered. I was spinning at an unnaturally fast rate, and descending at a very high speed. Try as I might
I couldn't overcome the centrifugal force which kept me anchored to my seat, and no amount of pulling with my hands on the sides of the cockpit would overcome it. Again and again I tried until quite unexpectedly I floated out of the cockpit... I was free, but only for a second or two. I was blown on to the remnants of the shattered tail unit where I stuck fast. I twisted, and turned, kicked and fought with every ounce of my strength until I finally broke free.

Instinctively I reached for the parachute rip-cord handle and it was then that I realised that my parachute had been partially torn from my back. The handle was not in its usual place and the whole parachute was whirling around my head as I tumbled over and over, the ground uncomfortably close. I can distinctly remember saying to myself at this juncture, 'Fancy being killed this way.' Meaning, of course, not in combat.

When all seemed lost, my parachute miraculously opened of its own accord – partially as it turned out – and only just in time, for a I seemd to hit the ground at the same moment. I was horizontal when I struck and this position, coupled with the fact that I ended up in a farmer's cess-pool which cushioned the impact, probably saved my life. I very nearly drowned in the foul stuff (but, in the circumstances, perhaps sweet!) as with a badly injured back making it agony to move. I had the greatest difficulty crawling free. A passing motorist came to my assistance, and together with his wife, helped me into his car and was good enough to drive me back to Catterick.

I was rushed off to hospital in the station ambulance and an immediate X-ray revealed no breaks, but disclosed a chipped coccyx. The damned thing has been a nuisance ever since...

Sergeant Squires' aircraft had caught fire on impact but he had full control and was able to bale out successfully, landing uninjured. On his first operational trip he was shot down by flak and taken prisoner-of-war."

(Alan C. Deere: *Nine Lives*, 1959)

Left: Mr J.R. Woods, Divisional, Safety Officer, ICI Billingham, during the war years and first leader of Teesside's "Maquis".
(Evening Gazette)

Right: Mr G.F. Guthrie, Stockton garage proprietor and member of Teesside's "Maquis". *(Evening Gazette)*

In the summer of 1940, when invasion seemed imminent, the foundations of local underground resistance movements were being laid throughout the country. The man chosen to establish the South Durham "cell" of seven men was a 56-year-old grey-haired and bespectacled Divisional Safety Officer of ICI Billingham, Mr J.R. Woods. In October 1940, he was sent for training at the Guerilla Warfare Centre, Coleshill, Wiltshire. What he studied there was not entirely new to him: he had already experienced that type of activity while serving with the Auxiliary Police Division in Ireland in the 1920s.

On his return to Teesside he ultimately selected five men to join him – but only after they had each been carefully vetted by the police (who were never told the purpose of the enquiries they were instructed to make). His sixth choice was made later. The existence of the group was so highly secret that for a long time the individuals composing it did not know each other's identity and members' families were totally unaware of what their menfolk were up to. Even when suspicious wives accused their husbands of "pubbing it" every night – when, in fact, those nights were spent perfecting techniques of sabotage and disruption – the accusers were never told the truth.

The trainees spent much time learning their trade. As Woods later explained: "We trained night and day in all kinds of conditions until we knew the countryside like our own back gardens. We were expert saboteurs and the Germans would have found bridges disappearing under their feet. Their sentries would have been under constant fear of death and their ammunition dumps would never have been safe."

The group needed an operational base, should the threat of invasion become reality, and Woods finally selected part of the woodlands on Lord Londonderry's Wynyard estate as the site for his secret HQ. He chose the site because he believed that, following a successful invasion, the Germans would choose the estate as their District Headquarters, that they would use the woodlands for the storing of tanks and ammunition, and that their General Staff would occupy the house. Woods and his team would be literally under their targets!

In conditions of the highest security, a team of Royal Engineers constructed a steel-lined underground chamber deep in the woods, equipped it with arms and ammunition and provisioned it with a month's supply of food and water. Entry was by a surface trapdoor that was so well camouflaged that its existence was undetectable to the uninformed, even when they were standing within feet of it. Some ten yards away was an escape exit – equally well hidden – to be used only in an emergency. It was while the bunker was being constructed that Woods recruited his sixth man. He was a Stockton garage proprietor and taxi-driver, G.F. Guthrie, who had frequently ferried Woods from the latter's home in Bank Road, Billingham, to Wynyard without ever guessing that he was chauffeur to Teesside's Maquis leader.

Thankfully, those men who were willing to take upon themselves a dangerous and onerous task when all seemed lost, never had to practise their deadly skills. However, their gesture is worthy of note. It is assumed that all of them are now dead, and if that is so then their exploits will probably go unrecorded and unsung. But somewhere deep below the trees of Wynyard Park there lies a dark and crumbling monument to more dangerous times, and to anonymous men who were willing to risk all to confront the threat that – had it become reality – would have touched us all.

At 7.55pm on Sunday, 13th October, 1940, a single German aircraft dropped four 250lb high-explosive bombs on the Marsh Road area of Middlesbrough and caused severe damage to properties in Benjamin Street, Hatherley Street, Nixon Street, Hartington Street, Marsh Road, Argyle Street, Farrar Street, Jamieson Street and Cannon Street. In the seconds that it took for those explosives to blast their way through that community 15 houses were totally demolished; 37 were rendered so dangerous that they would have to be pulled down; 38 were reduced to a state so unsafe that they would have to be evacuated; and a further 100 were badly damaged. In addition, a further 300 properties sustained damage of a lesser nature. The material cost of the attack was high, but the human cost was far higher: 20 dead, of whom four died after admission to hospital; 32 seriously injured and 72 with minor injuries. A number of people had remarkable escapes that evening, including an ARP worker and his family of four who had sought the protection offered by the cast-iron shelter at the junction of Marsh Road and Farrar Street. When the second bomb landed close to their refuge the ferocity of the blast blew out both ends of the shelter and catapulted the entire family out of one end. They escaped with scratches: other occupants were killed.

Top: The cast-iron shelter at the junction of Marsh Road and Farrar Street in which one family had a narrow escape. *(Cleveland County Archives)*

Left: The backs of the houses in Argyle Street. Numbers 71 to 97 were either demolished by blast or had to be pulled down subsequently. *(Cleveland County Archives)*

2nd November, 1940. Military personnel examine the wreckage of a German Ju.88 bomber which had crashed on the North Yorkshire moors the previous evening. The aircraft, of III/KG30 "Adler Geschwader" based at Eindhoven (Holland), was en route to attack the aerodrome at Linton-on-Ouse. It encountered fog over land and flew low over Glaisdale before striking the steep hillside at Glaisdale Head. The crew of four did not survive and were subsequently buried in Royal Air Force plot in Thornaby cemetery.
(E. Baxter/Evening Gazette)

Christmas, 1940. Alderman C. Harris (Mayor) and his daughter Audrey (Mayoress) attend festivities provided for members of the Armed Forces by the Redcar Salvation Army. The striking thing about this photograph is the number of grim faces on it. Whether this is a comment on the programme of entertainment provided or upon the (then) current international situation is not clear! Alderman Harris was destined not to survive the war: he was killed on 21st October, 1941, when a German bomb struck the Zetland Club, Coatham Road, Redcar. *(Cleveland County Libraries)*

Right: The blacksmith forges £s into armaments during Middlesbrough's War Weapons Week, 8th–15th March, 1941, when Middlesbrough War Savings Committee set itself the target of raising £1,000,000 to finance the building of three destroyers. *Far right:* In March, 1941, one of the "raids" on Middlesbrough came not from the Luftwaffe but from the RAF. As part of the town's "War Weapons' Week", RAF bombers showered leaflets over the area in an attempt to encourage the populace to finance the war effort through the purchase of War Bonds, Savings Certificates and Savings Stamps. The dropping of such leaflets was part of a week-long programme of concentrated fund-raising which also included the following attractions: orchestral concerts in the Town Hall and local cinemas, as well as open-air concerts in a variety of locations round town; parades of military and civil defence personnel; exhibitions of war artefacts, including a captured enemy aircraft and unexploded bombs; an exhibition of war paintings; a military PE display; flying displays by the RAF and displays of gun-drill by local Ack-Ack personnel; window competitions for local traders to promote interest in the fund-raising; and publicity film displays from National Savings Committee cinema vans which toured the area. *(Author's Collection)*

WAR WEAPONS WEEK · MIDDLESBROUGH

MARCH 8-15

ERIMUS

DIARY OF EVENTS

The Mayor extends to YOU an invitation to keep these 'engagements.'

Middlesbrough War Weapons Week

R.A.F. LEAFLET RAID

THIS MIGHT HAVE BEEN A BOMB!

By courtesy of "Evening Gazette"

LEND FREELY TO POUND HITLER *INSTEAD!*

££££££££££££££

March, 1941. A fanfare greets a procession of civic dignitaries – led by a local policeman and headed by the 2nd Marquis of Zetland (right) and the Mayor of Redcar Ald. C. Harris (left) – as they near the platform in the High Street from where the Marquis will declare open the town's War Weapons Week. The brick building to the right is the Presbyterian Church: the *Central* Cinema provides the background. *(Northern Echo)*

Film star Jack Warner signs an autograph for a young admirer during his visit to Redcar for the March 1941 War Weapons Week.
(Cleveland County Libraries)

A large crowd gathers in Redcar High Street in March 1941 to hear the 2nd Marquis of Zetland open the town's War Weapons Week. The building to the left of the National Provincial Bank is the Presbyterian Church. Note the public air raid shelter (mid-left), its entrance protected by a high brick wall, and the static water-tank immediately in front of it. Such reservoirs were scattered throughout urban centres to provide fire-fighting services with supplementary sources of water should these be needed. *(Cleveland County Libraries)*

Jack Warner shakes hands with the Mayor of Redcar, Alderman C. Harris, while keeping a keen eye on the camera. Also included in the group are: H. Caldwell (Town Clerk), R. Smith (Managing Clerk), W. Wardman, H. Spellman (Borough Treasurer), and Owen Walters (Band Leader). *(Cleveland County Libraries)*

Oberfeldwebel Beier of I/NJG2, a Luftwaffe night-fighter intruder unit, who claimed to have shot down a Boulton-Paul Defiant near Thornaby on the night of 13th June, 1941. (Simon Parry: *Intruders over Britain*, Air Research Publications 1987, p79.)

Feldwebel (Sgt) Peter Stahl, a Junkers 88 pilot of Kampfgeschwader 30, who believed that he and his crew carried out a lone attack on Middlesbrough on the night of 26th/27th April, 1941, after diverting from Hull, which was blanketed by cloud. He described the event thus:

"In the end I just have to give up (over Hull) and fly northwards in the hope of finding better visibility. Over Middlesbrough we can finally orientate ourselves beyond question, and I make my bombing run on the town... The AA defences are only moderate so that we can drop our explosive load quite accurately. On the way out, Hein and Theo report the flaring up of a fire... During our return flight over the North Sea I contemplate the sense or otherwise of such attacks. While I can rely on Hans to make every effort to find an important military target for our bombs, I also know that our terrible ammunition may have been unloaded somewhere where it would have no effect at all. Then again, what if it has hit a residential district or even a hospital? This war really is a gruesome business."
(P. Stahl: *The Diving Eagle*, Kimber, 1984.)

A national survey of people's attitudes to the various types of shelter, conducted soon after the outbreak of the war, showed that a majority favoured the "Anderson" – a construction of corrugated steel which was buried in the ground and which had two to three feet of soil on top of it. Their principal disadvantage seems to have been that water did tend to accumulate in them. As one respondent put it, "...a person is more likely to die from pleurisy by staying in one than by being bombed...". The efficiency of the "Morrison" – "...little more than a steel table with wire strung around it for use in the home..." – was distrusted by half of the respondents, while others considered brick street shelters to be "...about as much use as sick headache...".

That the latter statement was something of an exaggeration is borne out by the following photographs. Like all shelters of the period, those on the surface would not survive a direct hit, but they would usually stand up to the effects of blast – so long as the explosion was not too near!

Top: The effects of blast on a street shelter in Queen Mary Street, Middlesbrough, after a raid during the night of 16th May, 1941. Such was the power of the explosion that the middle section of the building was lifted off its foundations. Two women and three children who were inside at the time suffered only minor injuries. *(Middlesbrough Community History Project)*

Bottom: This shelter withstood the combined effects of blast and flying debris – but one cannot help thinking that it was a close run thing. (Date and precise location unknown but believed to be the Foxheads area, Newport, Middlesbrough, May, 1941.) *(Middlesbrough Community History Project)*

In the summer of 1941, Tom Sawyer was a Squadron Leader flying Halifax bombers with 76 Squadron, based at Middleton St. George. On 20th June, 1941, he had a narrow escape from disaster in the skies over Teesside.

"I took my first Halifax 1 on an operation on the night of 20th June. Kiel was the target, but I nearly didn't get there because it almost ended before it had begun. Middleton St. George was situated about ten miles from the centre of Middlesbrough, and this industrial town and port was protected against enemy attack with balloons besides the normal AA guns and searchlights.

"Having taken off at dusk on a clear summer evening, we made a wide circle inland before I set the course given to me by our navigator. Concentrating intently on the instruments and cockpit adjustments with my head down in the 'office' to make sure that everything was in order, I had just lined up the compass to the correct heading when Butch Heaton at the wireless set suddenly called out over the intercom: 'We're heading into the balloon barrage, Skipper' – and at almost the same moment I heard in my earphones the alarming high-pitched buzz of the 'squeakers' which indicated that we were indeed flying close to the balloons. This warning device was broadcast from the ground where the balloons were being flown, on the same frequency as our R/T, and supposedly to warn us that we were approaching a balloon defended area. The range was very limited for obvious reasons, and in this case was so short that we were in amongst the balloons before we picked up the warning.

"We were then flying at 4,000 feet, and glancing upwards I saw those damn great fat balloons sitting there about 7–800 feet above us, and clearly visible in the setting sun, although the ground below was in dark shadow. I couldn't see the cables, of course, but the balloons themselves indicated the direction of the wind since they naturally all pointed on the same heading, and I edged gingerly to one side to fly exactly between two balloons ahead of us in that particular line. They were fairly wide apart and there was room enough but it felt rather a tight squeeze at the time. Then, following the direction they were all pointing, I eased between the next two, and then the next, with my eyes glued upwards and climbing as steeply as I dared to try and get above the brutes, and finally breaking clear almost level with the last one, giving a cheerful 'All Clear' to the rest of my crew who had been suffering in silence while I had been juggling cautiously to get out of it. I realised that I was soaked with sweat as we settled down on course and began to relax, although there had been no physical exertion at all... The rest of the trip was a piece of cake by comparison."
(Group Capt. Tom Sawyer: *Only Owls and Bloody Fools Fly at Night*, Kimber, 1982.)

Above: On 19th June, 1941, King George VI and Queen Elizabeth made a surprise visit to Middlesbrough. As soon as their Majesties' visit became known, thousands of people flocked to vantage points and gave the royal couple a great welcome. They were greeted by large crowds when they arrived at Albert Park to inspect members of the local Civil Defence Services before going on to visit Thornaby aerodrome. During their short stay in the town, the King and Queen were escorted by the Mayor and Mayoress of Middlesbrough, Councillor Sir William and Lady Crosthwaite. *(Author's Collection)*

Left: Whitley bombers over Cleveland, c.1941. Middleton St. George aerodrome (known locally as Goosepool, after a nearby farm) was officially opened in January 1941 as a bomber station in No. 4 Group, Bomber Command. It had a decoy airfield at Crathorne, a few miles to the south-east. In April 1941, 16 Whitleys of 78 Squadron arrived from Dishforth and that same month made raids on enemy shipping and against Berlin. In October of that year, Croft was brought into use as a satellite airfield and 78 Squadron moved there with the old Whitleys and began to convert to Halifax bombers.
(Cleveland County Libraries)

Teesside's role as a major centre for shipbuilding and ship repairs has long since faded, but in earlier times the situation was far different. During the Second World War the Tees' yards of Furness Shipbuilding (Haverton Hill) and Smith's Dock Company (South Bank), together with William Gray's yard at Hartlepool, were thrown into a fervour of activity producing large numbers of naval vessels, including landing barges and frigates. The photograph left shows the Royal Navy frigate *Rother*, launched at Smith's Dock, 20th November, 1941, undergoing sea trials off the river Tees. The vessel was scrapped at Troon in April 1955. The picture below shows a partly submerged destroyer awaiting repair at Smith's. The date of the photograph is unknown – as is the name of the ship. *(Cleveland County Libraries)*

Opposite: In the early evening of 15th January, 1942, Holland-based bomber aircraft of KG2 launched attacks against shipping and port installations along England's eastern seaboard. Among those taking part was a Dornier 217E-4 of III/KG2 crewed by Feldwebel Joachim Lehnis (pilot), Lieutnant Rudolf Matern (bombardier), Unteroffizier Hans Maneke (radio-operator) and Oberfeldwebel Heinrich Richter (gunner). Lehnis had been ordered to attack a convoy which was travelling "eastwards of Middlesbrough", and it may well be that he was responsible for the bombing of the *Empire Bay*, which was bombed and seriously damaged further down the coast before it sank in Tees Bay. Between 5.30pm and 6.00pm he also bombed Skinnigrove Ironworks and Eston Jetty before colliding with a barrage balloon cable over Cargo Fleet works. The collision ripped off the aircraft's starboard wing and the Dornier plummeted into a coal yard in Clay Lane, South Bank. There were no survivors. The above list records their failure to return from operations: their deaths were confirmed three months later. *(Author's collection)*

III./Kampfgeschwader 2

Lfd. Nr.	Ort u. Tag des Verlustes	Staffel usw.	Dienstgrad	Vorname	Familienname, Truppenteil, Nr. der Erkennungsmarke	Geburts- Tag	Ort	Kreis	Gef.
1	2	3	4	5	6	7	8	9	
1.	ostw. Middles-brough. 15.1.1942 17.30 Uhr Do 217 E-4 Werk-Nr. 5314	8.	Feldw. aktiv F	Joachim	Lehnis 8./K.G. 2 69 642 32	18. 6. 18	Danzig		v
2.		8.	Leutnant d.R. B	Rudolf	Matern 8./K.G. 2 58 209 15	20. 8. 17	Paderborn	Westfalen	
3.		8.	Uffz. d.R. BF	Hans	Maneke 8./K.G. 2 57 359 75	26. 4. 18	Berlin Tegel		
4.		8.	Ofw. aktiv BM	Heinrich	Richter 8./K.G. 2 7. U.G. 3 63	16. 7. 11	Herisch- dorf Kr. Hirsch- berg		

Newport Road, looking towards Corporation Road, c.1940. To the right stands Binns' department store, which was spectacularly destroyed by fire in March, 1942, and had to be demolished. A more recent structure now occupies the site. Alongside is the Grand Electric cinema with its glittering lower facade of green Bakerlite edged with chrome. Fondly remembered by children of the 1940s/1950s as the location of so many Saturday morning triumphs of cowboy heroes – Roy Rogers, Gene Autrey, The Durango Kid – the "Electric" showed its last film on 8th April, 1961, before being demolished to make way for shops and Gas Board showrooms. During the subsequent decades the pace of redevelopment accelerated and most of the buildings shown in this photograph followed the Grand Electric into oblivion. *(Paul Stevenson Collection)*

March 28th, 1942. The fire-scarred shell of Binns department store stands roofless and floorless on the corner of Linthorpe Road and Newport Road. The blaze, which had raged for six hours the previous evening and which had been watched by large crowds, required the efforts of 350 firemen of the NFS using 48 appliances to bring it under control. Their demand for water outstripped hydrant supplies, which had to be supplemented by pumping additional sources from the nearby municipal swimming baths and from the River Tees, almost a mile away. Initially, the cause of the outbreak was considered to have been accidental. However, in June, Dickson and Benson's department store, in Dundas Street, and "Cheap Wilson's", in Corporation Road, suffered similar fates; in the same month, Upton's, at Garnet Street corner, was set on fire.
There was growing scepticism that the outbreaks were, in fact, accidental but it was not until some weeks later that the cause was finally ascertained – when a young schoolboy was discovered pushing burning paper through the letterbox of another store. *(Middlesbrough Community History Project)*

Wardens' Post

Official Bulletin of the
Middlesbrough Civil
Defence Wardens' Service

Under the Patronage of the
Chairman of the Civil Defence
Emergency Committee,
The Worshipful The Mayor
(Coun. SIR WM. CROSTHWAITE, J.P.)

APRIL
1942

Price 2d. Monthly

Middlesbrough's balloon barrage flies over the town while fuel tanks (at ICI Billingham?) continue to burn following the previous night's air raid on a date unknown, but probably July 1942. Wright's Tower House stands out white against the pall of smoke which snakes its way over the tall chimneys of the Ironmasters' District. The office of the Constantine Shipping Company (foreground) in Borough Road is surmounted by a small brick shelter from which aircraft spotters would sound the alarm in the event of imminent attack during daylight hours. *(Author's collection)*

In the early hours of Sunday, 26th July, 1942, the wail of sirens, the dropping of flares and the roar of gunfire provided the overture to what was to be the town's most destructive air-raid. Enemy planes attacked in relays and dropped high-explosives, oil bombs and hundreds of incendiaries, seemingly with the intention of setting the town ablaze. The NFS were soon attending 16 fires, three of which were designated as being "large". It was on this night that the Victoria Hall, the Co-op Emporium and Eaton's store were burned to the ground and the Leeds Hotel was destroyed by a direct hit. The raid lasted for an hour: when it was over 16 people had been killed, 50 injured and some 200 people had been rendered homeless; 68 houses and 76 business premises had been destroyed and minor damage had been inflicted on a further 1,200 properties. Only two industrial premises suffered notifiable damage.

This picture shows bomb-damaged shops in Wilson Street some days after the attack of 26th July, 1942. The boarded-up building on the left is the Wellington Hotel, which still occupies the site. *(K. Hoole Collection)*

July, 1942. Middlesbrough Corporation bus-driver Ron Nelson and his conductor, Tommy James, pose for the camera while resting at the Levick Crescent terminus before commencing their run to the "Transporter via Linthorpe Road". Of particular interest are the white-painted mudguards, the partly masked windows and the almost totally masked sidelights – all sure indicators that the picture was taken during war-time.

Because of the Blackout Regulations, road vehicles were permitted only minimum lighting during the hours of darkness: sidelights were allowed to emit only the merest pin-pricks of light, while headlamps were heavily masked to ensure that only a feeble beam shone on the near-side kerb almost immediately in front of the vehicle. Bus interiors were subjected to similar controls: blue bulbs were used to produce a minimum of illumination and the upper halves of windows were stained a similar colour to reduce the amount of light detectable from the air.

Driving was very difficult in such circumstances and at the end of their shifts crews often felt as if their "eyes were on six-inch stalks". The situation was worse in fog or during those times when the town's smoke defences were being used in anticipation of a raid: on those occasions the conductor would sometimes perch himself on the front near-side mudguard and call directions to the driver through the cab's side window.

If a raid did occur during a journey, the bus would stop at the nearest shelter so that passengers could take cover. If the crew intended to follow suit, the driver would remove the steering-wheel and take it with him. That was particularly the case in the early days of the war – when the threat of invasion was very real.

Because of the system of split shifts, bus crews could start work at 6am and might not finish until 11pm – a long day by any standards! In 1942, a driver's pay for a 60-hour week was £5 17s 3d gross; £4 12s 6d net. *(R. Nelson)*

July, 1942. One of a number of Spitfires purchased from subscriptions donated by the people of Middlesbrough during the war is made ready to join its squadron. The town's name and coat of arms can be clearly seen on the front fuselage. At the time of writing, nothing was known about the fate of this particular aircraft: more is known about the first Spitfire to be purchased by the town.

Throughout the period 1939–45, schemes to raise funds to finance the war effort were constantly being introduced by the national government and by local communities. Perhaps one of the first to be initiated locally was in 1940, when the then chairman of the Middlesbrough Motor Club, Bill Oliver, proposed a scheme to provide the Royal Air Force with a Spitfire which would bear the town's name and coat of arms. The estimated cost was some £5,000. The target sum was soon exceeded. On 20th November, during the course of a light supper organised by the Motor Club, Bill Oliver presented the Mayor with a cheque for £5,700, made payable to the Ministry of Aircraft Production.

The town's first Spitfire (R7122) was purchased early in 1941. On 1st June of that year it was issued to the newly formed 123 Squadron, RAF, based at Turnhouse (now Edinburgh airport). The squadron became operational on 8th June and was initially engaged on shipping patrols in and out of the Firth of Forth. On 9th July, 1941, the aircraft was damaged beyond repair in aerial combat, having been in service for only five weeks. *(A.W. Zealand)*

October, 1942. Sgt pilot F.E. Jones, 249 Squadron, RCAF, at the controls of the Spitfire purchased by the citizens of Darlington. *(Evening Gazette)*

The cheque that purchased Middlesbrough's first Spitfire for the RAF. *(A.W. Zealand)*

Middlesbrough Motor Club chairman, Bill Oliver (left), presenting the cheque for £5,700 to the Mayor of Middlesbrough, Cllr Sir William Crosthwaite. *(A.W. Zealand)*

Bank Holiday Monday, 3rd August, 1942, shortly after a low-flying Dornier 217 had aimed four 500kg bombs at Middlesbrough station. Two of the bombs scored direct hits and caused much damage to the structure but only slight damage to the lines. Freight traffic was moving through Middlesbrough within 25 hours of the attack and passenger traffic some eight hours after that. Sadly, eight people were killed and 58 injured. Strangely, the raider, which had crossed the coast just north of Saltburn, flew over virtually every target of any strategic importance in the Tees area before bombing what was, perhaps, the least important of all. The evidence suggests that the raider escaped. *(Northern Echo)*

The Dornier 217 made its first appearance over Britain in 1942. In fact, it was such an aircraft that collided with a balloon cable over Cargo Fleet and crashed into a coal yard at South Bank. It was also such an aircraft that carried out the low-level attack on Middlesbrough railway station. People who witnessed that attack saw a sight very similar to this as the raider swept low over the station canopy. *(Author's collection)*

7th August, 1942. Middlesbrough schoolchildren undergo gas drill in the Russell Street area during an ARP exercise. One of the principal points to emerge from the practice was the fact that many of the town's populace had ceased to carry their masks. They had to pay the penalty when they were caught by clouds of gas which were released in congested parts of the town. Several hundreds of people were queuing outside the *Odeon*, Corporation Road, when a cloud was relased near there. At least two-thirds of them did not have respirators. A number made a dash for safety, but others had to suffer acute discomfort for several minutes after being caught in the cloud and inhaling its contents. Their comments about the ARP are not known! *(E. Baxter/Evening Gazette)*

Tees-siders
WE NEED STILL MORE WAR SAVINGS
IF WE ARE TO ACHIEVE OUR OBJECTIVE——
25 TANKS for ATTACK

OUR 'LADS' NEED MORE TANKS...

Save FOR THE TANKS THEY ASK FOR

Women were given the option of entering one of the Women's branches of the Armed Forces or of taking "directed" employment (which would release men for active service). Mrs J. Turner of Stockton (front row; third from right) chose the latter. She was employed as a furnace-worker at Dorman Long's Bowesfield Lane Works, Stockton, where, as one of a team of four women, she pre-heated iron sheets prior to their being corrugated for use in the production of air-raid shelters. The women's work was always arduous but apparently eased as experience taught more effective techniques of handling. They worked a three-shift system and a six-day week for a weekly wage of £2. *(Mrs J. Turner)*

On the night of 15th/16th May, 1943, Dornier 217 bombers of KG2, based at Soesterberg, Holland, launched an attack on Sunderland. The raid was officially described as "heavy". During the course of attack the Luftwaffe lost one aircraft, which fell to the guns of a Beaufighter of 604 Squadron, based at Scorton. The aircraft plunged straight into the sea some 30 miles east of Sunderland and it is not known whether any of its crew managed to bale out before impact. The pilot was 23-year-old *Unteroffizier* Karl Roos, whose body was washed up on the beach at Blackhall Rocks on 30th June, 1943. The scene depicted is believed to be that of Roos' funeral at the Acklam Road cemetery, Thornaby, where the RAF had its own burial plot. As was the custom of the time, Karl Roos was buried with full military honours. *(Author's collection)*

During the war years, the tug-boats of the Tees Towing Company were rarely idle for any length of time. In addition to the services required by commercial shipping, the crews of those "workhorses" of the river were also kept busy with salvage work arising from enemy action as well as dealing with ships of the Royal and Allied Navies, which were regular visitors to the port. Such vessels ranged from large destroyers to landing-craft, the latter increasingly in evidence during 1943/1944 as the build-up to the Normandy landings gathered momentum. Perhaps the strangest tow which the tugs had to provide during those years was for two concrete caissons (code-named "Phœnix") which formed part of the Mulberry Harbour used to aid the D-Day landings. The photograph shows the first of the caissons, built at William Gray's Drydock, Graythorpe, in 1944, being manoeuvred out of the drydock prior to being towed to the southern assembly point by Royal Navy tugs. *(W. Haig Parry)*

Above, left: 1945. Olive Coulson proudly wears her VES Northern Command badge and her YMCA North East War Worker badge. *(Olive Coulson)*

Above, right: Olive Coulson (centre) poses on stage with Fire Service officers and other artistes at a war-time Christmas Party Concert at the Fire Service Administrative Centre, Wynyard Hall. The group includes Harold Peacock, Olive's partner in *The Aristocrats* (third left); Jack Mendelson, cartoonist (second right); Mr Morrison, zither (first right); Mabel Thorman, piano-accompanist (front right). *(Olive Coulson)*

Left: 1988. Olive with a 1945 concert poster which places her at the top of the bill. *(Whitby Gazette)*

When the war broke out, Olive Coulson was already well-established in local operatic circles, being a member of Stockton's (then well-known) Brunswick Church Choir, a winner of a number of northern eistoddfods, and occasional singer on BBC radio. In September, 1939, her career took on a new dimension, that of troop entertainer, when she was asked to sing at a troop concert at the town's YMCA, which was sited in the Temperance Hall. It was the first of some 700 such concerts she was to give during the course of the war.

At about the same time, she was invited to join a local Concert Party *(The Searchlights)* which was being formed to entertain the troops of Northern Command as part of the Voluntary Entertainment Service (V.E.S.). *The Searchlights*, which was formed by Billy Scarrow, who ran a pierrot show on Redcar beach before the war, had a number of well-known local artistes including Harry Whitcomb (comedian), Pat Fox (baritone), and Billy Burdon, another Redcar beach entertainer, who did a double act with Scarrow that had "...the soldiers really howling with laughter..." Olive used to sing solo, as well as in duet with Harold Peacock (when they were billed as *The Aristocrats*). Initially, the party travelled in two buses – one for the full orchestra which used to accompany the artistes – until transport difficulties caused the orchestra to be dropped.

In addition, Olive continued her voluntary work for the Stockton YMCA and visited all of the local gun-sites with other entertainers. Usually they performed in front of a full house, but many were the times that an alarm-bell warned of incoming raiders and Olive found herself singing to only a couple of soldiers who were off duty.

When the war was over, she sang at a number of *Welcome Home* concerts, but one occasion in particular stands high in her memory: "the wonderful *Thank You* concert for Northern Command artistes which was held in Saltburn Spa on 15th August, 1945."

All of the performers who had helped out during the war did a spot on the show and in a hall that was filled to capacity. Among the songs featured by *The Aristocrats* were: *With a song in my heart*; *Smoke gets in your eyes*; *At the balalaika*; and *I'll see you again*.

Olive readily admits that she enjoyed the war "singing-wise", but the reality of the conflict had never been far away. She remembers attending a concert held at the Bailey Street Schools, Stockton, for troops ("I thought they were only kids") destined to go overseas the next day. "We had a fantastic night, just singing together... A long time afterwards, I learned that they had all been killed going out... Somehow you don't forget.".

THE MISSIONS TO SEAMEN

MIDDLESBROUGH

GRAND

VARIETY CONCERT

(arranged by Jack Mendelson)

BY ARTISTES OF THE
NORTHERN COMMAND

TUESDAY, 30th MARCH, 1943

commencing 7-30 p.m.

PROGRAMME

MABEL THORMAN	Piano Solo
DOROTHY SMURTHWAITE	Popular Songstress
JACK MENDELSON	Cartoonist
MOLLY HILTON	Zylophonist and Speciality Dancer
FRED HAY	Yodeller
PAT SYMINGTON	Vocalist and Dancer
ERNIE O'BRIEN	Comedian
OLIVE COULSON	B.B.C. Contralto, Gold Medallist
FRED PROBEE	Mimic
At the Piano	MABEL THORMAN
Compere:	T. HILTON

County Borough of Middlesbrough

To

WILLIAM NORMAN   C.D. Warden

This Certifies — that you have served your fellow citizens with unselfish credit and unassuming distinction, and have undertaken loyal service to our beloved country during our time of peril from enemy air raids in the European War, 1939 to 1945. By your achievements and sacrifice of time and convenience you have earned the gratitude of the people of Middlesbrough.

The Middlesbrough Civil Defence Committee hereby acknowledges on behalf of the whole community their profound gratitude, warm appreciation and their most grateful thanks.

Chairman of the Civil Defence Committee.

Town Clerk and A.R.P. Controller

A Certificate of Service which was issued to all who had been members of the Civil Defence Forces during the war.

8th June, 1946

TO-DAY, AS WE CELEBRATE VICTORY, I send this personal message to you and all other boys and girls at school. For you have shared in the hardships and dangers of a total war and you have shared no less in the triumph of the Allied Nations.

I know you will always feel proud to belong to a country which was capable of such supreme effort; proud, too, of parents and elder brothers and sisters who by their courage, endurance and enterprise brought victory. May these qualities be yours as you grow up and join in the common effort to establish among the nations of the world unity and peace.

George R.I.

Schoolchildren received an acknowledgement of the fact that they too had "shared in the hardships and dangers of total war".

STOCKTON HIPPODROME

NEXT WEEK:

LESLIE BANKS and VIVIEN LEIGH
in
TWENTY-ONE DAYS
with LAURENCE OLIVIER
ELLIOT MASON ✦ ESME PERCY

Also Showing
WEST OF SANTA FE
Featuring CHARLES STARRETT
IRIS MEREDITH, DICK CURTIS.
UNIVERSAL NEWS.

THE PLAZA, Stockton — 5.45—CONTINUOUS—10.30. MONDAY NEXT.

FOR THREE DAYS ONLY.

Old Mother Riley in Paris
Also Don Terry and Rosalind Keith in A FIGHT TO THE FINISH.
Thursday.—THERE AIN'T NO JUSTICE.

CENTRAL HALL
6.15 — THORNABY — 8.30.
Monday, Tuesday, Wednesday.
The Lone Wolf's Daughter (U)
Starring Warren William and Ida Lupino.
Also Walter Abel in FIRST OFFENDERS (A)
Thurs., Fri., Sat. — ELEPHANTS NEVER FORGET (U) and BAREFOOT BOY (U).
Matinee on Monday and Thursday at 2.0.
Patrons must bring their Gas Masks.

QUEEN'S CINEMA
6.15 — THORNABY — 8.30.
Monday, Tuesday, Wednesday.
WALTER PIDGEON,
Virginia Bruce and Leo Carrillo in
SOCIETY LAWYER (A)
Also Robert Kent in CONVICTS' CODE (A).
Thurs., Fri., Sat.—THE HOUND OF THE BASKERVILLES (A)
Matinee on Monday and Thursday at 2.0 p.m.
Patrons must bring their Gas Masks.

GRAND ELECTRIC THEATRE
Middlesbrough. ALL NEXT WEEK.
The RITZ BROTHERS in **THE GORILLA** (H). | Also PRESTON FOSTER in **CHASING DANGER** (U)
Children under 16 not admitted, whether accompanied by adults or not.

EMPIRE MIDDLESBROUGH
'Phone 2346.

CLOSED ALL NEXT WEEK FOR PRODUCTION.
RE-OPENING XMAS NIGHT, DECEMBER 25th.
WITH WALTER PASKIN & ELKEN SIMONS' SUPER PANTOMIME—

ONCE NIGHTLY AT 6-45 — **ALADDIN** — ONCE NIGHTLY AT 6-45

A Delightful Christmas Entertainment specially adapted to meet the tastes of Young and Old alike.

Information regarding the 1939–45 period in the Teesside/Cleveland area is not easy to come by: written sources are meagre in the extreme; most information rests in the minds of those whose lives were touched by the events of the time. Thus my quest for personal recollections continues.

If there are readers of this volume who have experiences that they would be willing to share – or photographs that they would be willing to loan so that a copy might be taken – I should be very interested to hear from them. No incident should be considered too small: it is the small details that help to make the total picture possible.

Bill Norman,
23a Thames Avenue,
GUISBOROUGH,
Cleveland, TS14 8AE